Thinking Critically:
Mass Shootings

Stephen Currie

San Diego, CA

© 2023 ReferencePoint Press, Inc.
Printed in the United States

For more information, contact:
ReferencePoint Press, Inc.
PO Box 27779
San Diego, CA 92198
www.ReferencePointPress.com

LIBRARY OF CONGRESS CATALOGING-IN-PUBLICATION DATA

Names: Currie, Stephen, 1960- author.
Title: Thinking critically : mass shootings / by Stephen Currie.
Description: San Diego, CA : ReferencePoint Press, [2022] | Series:
    Thinking critically | Includes bibliographical references.
Identifiers: LCCN 2022005255 (print) | LCCN 2022005256 (ebook) | ISBN
    9781678203184 (library binding) | ISBN 9781678203191 (ebook)
Subjects: LCSH: Mass shootings--United States--Prevention--Juvenile
    literature. | Gun control--United States--Juvenile literature. | Mental
    health services--United States--Juvenile literature.
Classification: LCC HV6536.5 .C87 2022 (print) | LCC HV6536.5 (ebook) |
    DDC 364.152/340973--dc23/eng/20220211
LC record available at https://lccn.loc.gov/2022005255
LC ebook record available at https://lccn.loc.gov/2022005256

Contents

Foreword

"Literacy is the most basic currency of the knowledge economy we're living in today." Barack Obama (at the time a senator from Illinois) spoke these words during a 2005 speech before the American Library Association. One question raised by this statement is: What does it mean to be a literate person in the twenty-first century?

E.D. Hirsch Jr., author of *Cultural Literacy: What Every American Needs to Know*, answers the question this way: "To be culturally literate is to possess the basic information needed to thrive in the modern world. The breadth of the information is great, extending over the major domains of human activity from sports to science."

But literacy in the twenty-first century goes beyond the accumulation of knowledge gained through study and experience and expanded over time. Now more than ever literacy requires the ability to sift through and evaluate vast amounts of information and, as the authors of the Common Core State Standards state, to "demonstrate the cogent reasoning and use of evidence that is essential to both private deliberation and responsible citizenship in a democratic republic."

The Thinking Critically series challenges students to become discerning readers, to think independently, and to engage and develop their skills as critical thinkers. Through a narrative-driven, pro/con format, the series introduces students to the complex issues that dominate public discourse—topics such as gun control and violence, social networking, and medical marijuana. All chapters revolve around a single, pointed question such as Can Stronger Gun Control Measures Prevent Mass Shootings?, or Does Social Networking Benefit Society?, or Should Medical Marijuana Be Legalized? This inquiry-based approach introduces student researchers to core issues and concerns on a given topic. Each chapter includes one part that argues the affirmative and one part that argues the negative—all written by a single author. With the single-author format the predominant arguments for and against an issue can be synthesized into clear, accessible discussions supported by details and evidence including relevant facts, direct quotes, current examples, and statistical illustrations. All volumes include focus questions to guide students as they read each pro/con discussion, a list of key facts, and an annotated list of related organizations and websites for conducting further research.

The authors of the Common Core State Standards have set out the particular qualities that a literate person in the twenty-first century must have. These include the ability to think independently, establish a base of knowledge across a wide range of subjects, engage in open-minded but discerning reading and listening, know how to use and evaluate evidence, and appreciate and understand diverse perspectives. The new Thinking Critically series supports these goals by providing a solid introduction to the study of pro/con issues.

Mass Shootings in America

August 3, 2019, seemed like an ordinary Saturday in the city of El Paso, situated in the extreme western part of Texas along the Mexican border. Residents went about their business of soccer games, dance classes, housecleaning, and other routine activities, including shopping. One of the city's Walmart stores, located in a busy commercial part of El Paso, was especially crowded that morning as families and individuals looked for tools, housewares, school supplies, and more. Many of the shoppers were of Mexican descent, appropriate for a city where the majority of residents are Hispanic; some were residents of Mexico who had crossed the border that morning to look for bargains.

But it was not an ordinary Saturday at all. At about 10:40 a.m. a man walked into the Walmart brandishing a high-powered rifle and began shooting at shoppers. The store filled with smoke and the sounds of gunfire. Screams echoed off the store's walls. Customers and employees dived to the ground, hurried for the store's other exits, and hid in storage containers in hopes of evading the hail of bullets. El Paso resident Robert Jurado found shelter between two vending machines when the shooter fired in his direction. "That's where the individual tried to shoot at me," he said later, "[but] he missed 'cause I kind of ducked down."[1]

Not all shoppers that day were as fortunate. The shooter, a twenty-one-year-old White man from another Texas community several hundred miles away, wounded twenty-three people and killed twenty-three more, including several who died from their wounds after the actual shooting took place. "I saw people crying: children, old people, all in shock," says shopper Manuel Uruchurtu. "I saw a baby, maybe 6 to 8 months old, with blood all over their belly."[2] The shooter then returned to his car and drove away. At an intersection some distance from the store, he approached Texas law enforcement agents and surrendered, acknowledging that he was the killer. The shooter went on to explain that he was shooting specifically at Hispanics because he feared that they were taking over the United States. Indeed, he had published a manifesto online in which he wrote angrily about the ongoing "Hispanic invasion of Texas" and the "cultural and ethnic replace-ment"[3] of Whites by other groups.

A Now-Familiar Event

The El Paso shooting was a terrible tragedy—but one that is all too familiar to Americans. Dozens of other mass shootings have made headlines across the United States during the past few de-cades. Well-known incidents include a 2012 shooting at Sandy Hook Elementary School in Newtown, Connecticut, which killed twenty-seven, mostly young children; a shooting at a nightclub in Orlando, Florida, which killed forty-nine people in 2016; a shoot-ing at a music festival in Las Vegas, Nevada, in 2017, which killed sixty people; and a shooting at Marjory Stoneman Douglas High School in Parkland, Florida, in 2018, which killed seventeen. While the death toll at El Paso was high in comparison to many other events, it was hardly unprecedented; nearly thirty mass shootings over the years have resulted in at least ten fatalities.

Most mass killings in the United States follow a pattern, and in many ways the El Paso tragedy fits that pattern. Most obviously, the shooter was a man. Men carry out virtually all mass shootings; as scholar and researcher Jillian Peterson describes it, "Men just are generally more violent."[4] The El Paso shooter also acted alone, which is com-mon for mass shootings; though some mass shooters act in pairs, the great majority do not. In addition, the shooter was White, the race of slightly over half

> "Men just are generally more violent."[4]
>
> —Jillian Peterson, gun violence researcher

People mourn for the dead and wounded a day after a gunman opened fire inside a Walmart store in El Paso, Texas, in 2019. During the last few decades, mass shootings have become a depressingly familiar aspect of American life.

of mass shooters. Like most mass shooters, the El Paso gunman also planned his rampage carefully. He knew exactly where he wanted to go and when he would begin shooting—and he used a semiautomatic weapon that allowed him to fire off bullets at an extremely rapid pace.

There were some differences between the El Paso shooter and other gunmen, however. Most obviously, about 60 percent of mass shooters die at the scene of their crimes, either by committing suicide or by being shot and killed by police. The El Paso shooter, in contrast, left the scene before police officers arrived and did not take his own life. The racial motivation of the El Paso shooter, moreover, was somewhat unusual. Some other mass shooters have targeted individuals of a particular race or ethnicity. In early 2021, for instance, a shooter in Georgia killed several women of Asian descent, and in 2015 a shooter killed nine African Americans at a church in Charleston, South Carolina. But experts say mass shootings are more often motivated by a general anger at the world or at individual people rather than at a specific group.

Other similarities link mass shooters as well. Research by Peterson and others demonstrates that most mass shooters suffered major childhood trauma, such as physical or sexual abuse, the death of a parent, or bullying at the hands of classmates and other children in the neighborhood. For most mass shooters, moreover, the crime was immediately preceded by a significant event: the loss of a job, the end of a relationship, the death of a loved one. In addition, most mass shooters have showed deep interest in the experiences of earlier mass shooters, often copying their methods in addition to their goals. Finally, mass shooters generally have a history of violence. According to one study, more than 60 percent have had brushes with the law over violent behavior, with over a quarter having engaged in domestic violence.

The statistics on mass shootings are sobering. A research group called Gun Violence Archive has kept track of all mass shootings in the United States since 2013, when the group was founded. Using Gun Violence Archive's definition of mass shooting—in effect, an incident in which four or more people are wounded or killed by gunfire—there were over two thousand mass shootings from 2013 through 2020. (Domestic violence cases, gang warfare, and organized acts of terrorism are excluded from these figures.) That amounts to an average of close to one mass shooting per day. Even if more stringent definitions are used, mass shootings are all too common. Defining a mass shooting as resulting in four or more deaths rather than simply four or more wounded, the *Washington Post* concludes that from 2016 through 2020 there was one mass shooting every six or seven weeks.

Reactions

There is a broad consensus in the United States that mass shootings must be stopped. "My heart is with everyone in El Paso struck by this unspeakable evil,"[5] said Texas senator Ted Cruz in the wake of the Walmart shooting. Similar expressions of concern came from leaders across the political spectrum as well as from many ordinary Americans. There is much less consensus, however, regarding the root causes of these shootings—and as a result, much less consensus regarding the steps that need to be taken to ensure that such tragedies stop happening. Within hours of the El Paso shooting, for example, a debate began about the causes of the massacre and what the appropriate responses might be.

That debate over causes usually comes down to two possibilities: mental illness and access to guns. Texas governor Greg Abbott was among those who expressed the view that mental illness was the fundamental cause of this shooting and others. In the belief that the El Paso shooter and others like him can and should be identified as troubled before they pick up a gun and start shooting, Abbott advocated for better mental health care. Former US representative Beto O'Rourke—whose district had included El Paso—was among those who expressed the view that the central problem was not mental health but easy access to guns. Armed with a knife or a pipe wrench rather than a firearm, O'Rourke pointed out, the killer could not possibly have extinguished so many lives in so little time. In O'Rourke's view, the solution to mass shootings lay in reducing the availability of firearms.

Still others held different views. Texas lieutenant governor Dan Patrick and US House minority leader Kevin McCarthy, for example, both argued that violent video games were the problem. They advocated bans on the most violent of these games on the supposition that playing them incessantly desensitizes players to the realities of violence and makes them eager to engage in it themselves. And some observers blamed the violence in El Paso on anti-immigrant comments made by then-president Donald Trump. In their opinion, Trump's remarks normalized hatred and fear of non-White Americans and foreigners—especially people of Mexican descent.

> "It is past time to act. . . . Doing nothing is not an option."[6]
>
> —Tammy Baldwin, US senator

Whatever the reasons for mass shootings, the current situation is unsustainable. Gun Violence Archive counted twenty-five mass shootings in the month of January 2022 alone; estimates of the number of dead and wounded from mass shootings in 2021 exceed three thousand. As Wisconsin senator Tammy Baldwin put it after the mass shooting in Orlando, "It is past time to act. . . . Doing nothing is not an option."[6] Unfortunately, there is still no agreement on what solution is best—and thus no clear idea of how this horrible violence can be stopped.

Chapter One

Could Improvements in Mental Health Care Reduce Mass Shootings?

Improvements in Mental Health Care Can Significantly Reduce Mass Shootings

- A significant percentage of mass shooters are mentally ill.
- The United States needs more and better treatment for people who are mentally ill.
- Mentally ill people are being released from hospitals when they should not be.

The Debate at a Glance

Improvements in Mental Health Care Will Not Significantly Reduce Mass Shootings

- Most mass shooters are not mentally ill.
- The great majority of mentally ill people are not violent and not a threat to anyone.
- Increasing support for mental health is a worthwhile goal but will not stop mass shootings.

Improvements in Mental Health Care Can Significantly Reduce Mass Shootings

"Mental illness and hatred pull the trigger."

—Former US president Donald Trump

Quoted in Jillian Peterson and James Densley, *The Violence Project*. New York: Abrams, 2021, p. 59.

Consider these questions as you read:

1. How convincing is the argument that mass shootings could be greatly reduced through improved access to mental health care? Explain your answer.
2. In your opinion, what is the main reason for people not getting mental health help when they need it? Explain your answer.
3. Do you believe that mental illness combined with homelessness is a recipe for mass shootings? Why or why not?

Editor's note: The discussion that follows presents common arguments made in support of this perspective, reinforced by facts, quotes, and examples taken from various sources.

Mass shooters are linked by several important characteristics. They are overwhelmingly male. They are typically White and of working age; the bulk of mass shooters are ages twenty-one to fifty-four. When they were young, they had reputations as loners and were either bullies or were frequently bullied themselves. These characteristics are well known among those who study mass shootings—and those who watch the coverage of the latest mass killing on television or follow the story on the internet. But there is another distinction that many mass shooters share, one that may suggest a path toward reducing the number of mass killings. That characteristic is mental illness: schizophrenia, borderline personality disorder, or other conditions that affect the brain and interfere with a person's ability to reason, feel appropriate emotions, or form social relationships.

Shooters with Mental Illness

There is no question that many mass killers have displayed signs of mental illness. For example, a man who killed seven people in a rampage near Akron, Ohio, in 2011 was often seen sitting in a kayak on his front lawn under the impression that he was afloat. Another killer, who staged a mass shooting in 2013 at the Washington Navy Yard in the District of Columbia, took apart a bed in his hotel room in the belief that somebody was hidden beneath it. The man who shot Arizona representative Gabby Giffords and killed several others at a political event in 2011 also displayed behavior suggestive of mental illness. "Sometimes you'd hear him in his room, like, having conversations," reports his mother. "And sometimes he would look like he was having a conversation with someone right there, be talking to someone."[7] Psychiatric examination after that shooting, in fact, revealed that the murderer was too mentally ill to stand trial.

> "I told him he's living in a box right now and the box will only get smaller over time if he doesn't get some treatment."[9]
>
> —Psychiatric nurse regarding the Sandy Hook shooter

Other mass shooters never seemed quite so out of touch with reality but nonetheless gave the people around them reason to worry about their mental health. Several had been under psychiatric care at some point before they opened fire. One of many examples was the shooter who killed twelve people at a movie theater in Aurora, Colorado, in 2012. In his visits to a psychiatrist as a young adult, he revealed that he had "homicidal thoughts"[8] multiple times a day. Similarly, the man who murdered thirty-two people at Virginia Tech in 2007 was diagnosed with an extreme case of social anxiety disorder as a boy and was on psychotropic medication for several years. And a psychiatric nurse begged the parents of the Sandy Hook killer to put him on medication when he was fourteen. "I told him he's living in a box right now and the box will only get smaller over time if he doesn't get some treatment,"[9] says the nurse. But the boy's mother refused—with dreadful results several years later.

Mass Shooters with a Psychiatric Diagnosis

A 2021 Stanford University study of thirty-five mass shooters found that twenty-eight, or 80 percent, had been given a psychiatric diagnosis. Of this group, eighteen had schizophrenia. The other ten had various mental health issues including bipolar disorder, delusional disorders, and personality disorders. Clearly mental illness is an enormous driver of mass shootings, so it stands to reason that improved mental health care would reduce such shootings.

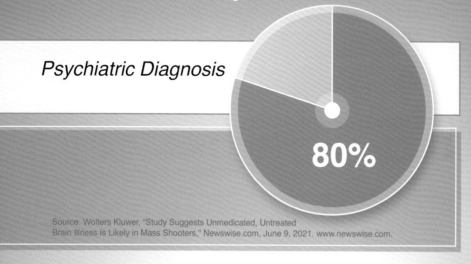

Psychiatric Diagnosis

80%

Source: Wolters Kluwer, "Study Suggests Unmedicated, Untreated Brain Illness Is Likely in Mass Shooters," Newswise.com, June 9, 2021. www.newswise.com.

Statistical Evidence

Indeed, recent research suggests that a large number of mass shooters have a mental illness when they carry out their killings or that they have experienced mental illness at some recent point in their lives. In 2019, for example, a study done by the National Council for Behavioral Health estimated that about one-third of mass shooters suffered from serious mental illness. In most cases, the authors of the study noted, little if anything had been done to alleviate the problem. A more recent study, published in 2021 by a team led by Ira Glick of the Stanford University School of Medicine, looked at thirty-five mass shootings in which the shooter survived. Glick's team concluded that twenty-eight of these shooters—a shocking 80 percent—had been given a psychiatric diagnosis.

"None were medicated or received other treatment prior to the crime,"[10] the researchers note.

Regardless of the actual number of mass shooters who are mentally ill, it is clear that mass shootings are disproportionately carried out by people with psychiatric problems. This evidence points to a straightforward solution: improve mental health care. No one expects to eliminate mass shootings altogether with this approach. But that is scarcely a reason not to try. As Glick's report states, "The psychiatric disorders seen in perpetrators of mass shootings are serious brain illnesses—as much in need of proper diagnosis and treatment as heart disease or any other medical condition."[11]

Room for Improvement

Certainly, mental health care in this country has plenty of room for improvement. America does not devote nearly enough resources to mental health. Studies indicate that less than half the Americans who need mental health care receive it. There are many reasons for this unfortunate situation. One is cost; although health insurance companies are increasingly willing to cover mental health treatment, many people are uninsured, and numerous mental health providers do not take insurance. Aside from that, there simply are not enough trained practitioners to address the nation's very large mental health needs. "Even with the number of psychiatrists and psychologists out there," says behavioral health expert Carol Alter, "there's nobody for people to go to."[12]

Another issue is that there is a stigma attached to mental health care in the United States. The prevailing belief is that people should be able to overcome problems on their own. Mental health professionals fight back against this idea. "Don't let the fear of being labeled with a mental illness prevent you from seeking help,"[13] advises the website of the prestigious Mayo Clinic in Rochester, Minnesota. Still, the stigma remains an issue.

In other ways, too, mental health offerings could be improved. Mental health services in public schools, for example, are sadly lacking. Nationwide there is one school counselor for every 464 students—a far cry from the ratio of one for every 250 advocated by the American School Counselor Association. Counselors responsible for more than 400 or 500 students cannot possibly get to know them well enough to identify those who may present a danger to themselves or others. Mental health coverage in public schools could be improved in other ways, too. "We do screening for vision and hearing," says psychologist Katie Eklund. "Why don't we do the same for social-emotional and mental health?"[14]

As for hospitals that treat the mentally ill, they are chronically underfunded and understaffed. That problem has been exacerbated by the COVID-19 pandemic. But even before the pandemic began, many hospitals routinely had fewer beds than mental health patients needing treatment.

> "We do screening for vision and hearing. Why don't we do the same for social-emotional and mental health?"[14]
>
> —Katie Eklund, psychologist

A final issue with mental health care today is the long-term trend of releasing patients with mental illness from hospitals. Society's zeal to help people resume normal lives has gone overboard. Many patients with serious mental issues have been removed from hospital care long before they were ready. Many wind up on the streets, often homeless, with no one to ensure that they take their medications. This is a recipe for creating a mass shooter. The solution is to devote more resources to mental health care: more money to psychiatric hospitals, more funding for mental health professionals, and a concerted effort to break down the stigma of receiving mental health care. Improving access to mental health care will not cure the problem of mass shootings, but it will go a long way toward fixing it. And it may be the only thing that can.

Improvements in Mental Health Care Will Not Significantly Reduce Mass Shootings

"The First Amendment protects free speech, including even the most unsettling fantasies, and no one has developed a way to discern who is the merely obsessed and who is the actually violent person."

—Author John Woodrow Cox

John Woodrow Cox, *Children Under Fire*. New York: HarperCollins, 2021, p. 39.

Consider these questions as you read:

1. Do you think mental illness as a cause of mass shootings has been exaggerated? Why or why not?
2. Does the focus on mental illness as the cause of mass shootings distract from other more important causes? Why or why not?
3. What are some of the other possible causes of mass shootings, and how important are these when compared to mental illness? Explain your answer.

Editor's note: The discussion that follows presents common arguments made in support of this perspective, reinforced by facts, quotes, and examples taken from various sources.

Improving mental health services throughout the United States is a fine idea. But suggestions that such improvements will significantly reduce the number of mass shootings are misguided. There is no way to know how many mass shootings have been carried out by people who are truly mentally ill. It is also unclear how many mentally ill mass shooters would have been deterred even with excellent psychiatric treatment.

Let us start with the assumption that significant numbers of mass shooters are mentally ill. It is easy to toss numbers around, but the truth is that no one really knows how many of these killers are mentally disturbed. Even those who accept the notion that mental health support might make a difference have no idea of the actual numbers. When a 2019 study suggests the figure is 33 percent and a 2021 study suggests 80 percent, it is clear that there is no definitive answer. In fact, other research suggests that these figures are considerably exaggerated. A 2020 study by Columbia University psychiatrist Gary Brucato, for example, concludes that just 8 percent of mass shooters have severe mental health issues. As Brucato notes, "Serious mental illness . . . as a risk factor for mass shootings is given undue emphasis."[15]

Indeed, while it is easy to find examples of mass shooters who had been in psychiatric care—or who clearly should have been—it is equally easy to find mass killers who were not motivated by delusions. "While a minority of these

> "Serious mental illness . . . as a risk factor for mass shootings is given undue emphasis."[15]
>
> —Gary Brucato, psychiatrist

shooters might have benefitted from treatment to reduce psychotic symptoms," writes physician Amy Barnhorst, "the majority appeared to be driven more by entitlement, misogyny, white supremacy, or a desire for revenge—conditions that are notoriously difficult to treat."[16] For example, the shooter in Charleston, South Carolina, was motivated by hatred for African Americans. Likewise, in 2021 authorities broke up a plot by an Ohio man to kill members of a college sorority because of what prosecutors called "hatred [of women], jealousy, and revenge."[17] Most workplace shootings, similarly, are less a random act of someone delusional than the intentional action of a person who has recently lost a job. It is simply not the case that most mass shootings are the result of a mental illness.

Increasing Support for Mental Health

At the same time, those who believe that mental health support would reduce mass shootings underestimate the difficulties of increasing that support. All we need to do, they seem to suggest, is find all people who have a serious mental illness and treat them; then no mentally ill person will ever again become a mass shooter. But people with a mental illness do not always want treatment, and in most cases society cannot force people into treatment unless they present an immediate physical threat to themselves or others. In Pennsylvania, for example, the law requires that a person be a "clear and present danger"[18] before it is acceptable to force the person into a mental health facility. That is a high standard, and it should be. It is important to weigh the rights of individuals against the risk to society, and in the United States we have chosen to err on the side of individual rights. We do not force people into psychiatric treatment simply because we think they *might* turn out to be mass shooters.

Moreover, the link between mental illness and mass shootings is tenuous at best. According to some estimates, up to 20 million Americans suffer from a serious mental illness. But only a tiny fraction of these individuals will ever attempt a mass shooting. That is because a mental illness does not cause violent behavior. In fact, the two are not closely linked. As a 2016 study carried out by physicians James L. Knoll IV and George D. Annas points out, "A person is about 15 times more likely to be struck by lightning in a given year than to be killed by a stranger with a diagnosis of schizophrenia or chronic psychosis."[19]

> "A person is about 15 times more likely to be struck by lightning in a given year than to be killed by a stranger with a diagnosis of schizophrenia or chronic psychosis."[19]
>
> —James L. Knoll IV and George D. Annas, physicians

Blaming Mental Health

At the same time, it is easy to blame these terrible crimes on a mental illness and those who have one. As Jim Windell of the Michigan Psychological Association notes, it is comforting to

A 2020 Columbia University study concludes that just 8 percent of mass shooters have a severe mental illness. Many more mass shooters are motivated by jealousy, anger, and revenge than by delusional thinking. This data strongly suggests that the connection between mass shooters and mental health is much less significant than commonly believed.

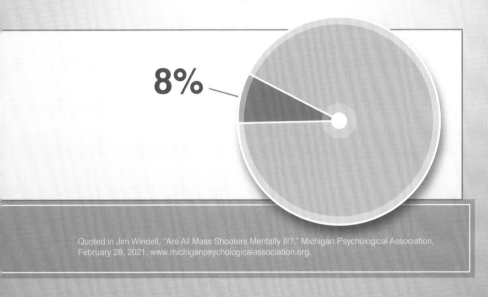

8%

Quoted in Jim Windell, "Are All Mass Shooters Mentally Ill?," Michigan Psychological Association, February 28, 2021. www.michiganpsychologicalassociation.org.

think that mentally ill people are responsible for the great bulk of mass shootings. "We don't have to think about why such tragic events happen or how society needs to change," Windell writes. "A mentally ill person who is responsible for a horrific tragedy can be locked away and we can go on with our lives."[20]

Windell's words indicate an important truth: not only are people with a mental illness being unfairly blamed for mass shootings, but the constant emphasis on mental illness turns public attention away from solutions that might actually be effective. Guns are a good example. Instead of looking strictly at the problem of mental illness, we could focus on reducing the number of guns in this country. We could limit sales of semiautomatic weapons or ensure that people who are likely to harm others do not have access to firearms. Any of these could be a truly effective way to reduce mass shootings.

More Solutions

There are other possible solutions to the problem of mass violence, too, which we sometimes ignore—in part because of the widespread emphasis on mental illness. For example, there is evidence that the great majority of mass shooters feel disconnected and alienated from the rest of society. That alienation might not be related to mental illness. Rather, it is an artifact of living in modern society. There may be ways of addressing this problem, but we will never find them if we are focused too heavily on mental illness. Similarly, we could take steps to reduce the impact of corrosive ideologies such as misogyny and White supremacy. Enough shooters are motivated by these ideologies that addressing this issue would yield better results than blaming mental illness.

Another change we might consider making is to reduce the attention we give to mass shootings, especially where the perpetrators are concerned. "Shooters get enormous attention," points out the National Center for Health Research. "This sometimes inspires a copycat shooting, where the potential shooter typically tries to kill more people than their predecessor." We know that many mass killers are influenced by earlier mass shootings. The Virginia Tech shooter in 2007, for example, wrote that he hoped to replicate the shootings in Columbine eight years earlier. What if the Columbine killers' names had not been plastered all over the news? "By reducing the fame and attention that mass shooters receive," concludes the center, "there will be fewer obsessive fans that become copycat shooters."[21]

Mass shootings are a real problem, and real problems need real solutions. But blaming mass violence on people who experience mental illness is not a solution. Doing so only serves to distract society from the true causes of mass shootings—and makes it that much more difficult to find effective responses to the problem. By all means, let us improve mental health services in our country. Let us make sure that people with violent delusions or compulsions get the treatment they need and deserve. To do so is kind, wise, and entirely appropriate. But let us not fool ourselves into thinking that doing so will make much of a dent in the numbers of mass shootings.

Chapter Two

Can Gun Control Measures Reduce Mass Shootings?

Gun Control Measures Will Reduce Mass Shootings

- Mass killings are essentially impossible without the presence of guns.
- Many people who currently own guns should not be permitted access to firearms.
- Some types of weapons are more powerful than anyone needs and should be banned.

The Debate at a Glance

Gun Control Measures Will Not Reduce Mass Shootings

- Historically and statistically, gun control measures are ineffective.
- Gun control measures would infringe on the rights of law-abiding citizens.
- Mass shooters can get guns even when they are not legally allowed to buy them.

Gun Control Measures Will Reduce Mass Shootings

"We can elect policy makers who . . . will pass the commonsense gun laws that the majority of Americans agrees will make it easier to keep guns away from people who shouldn't have them."

Mass shootings experts Jillian Peterson and James Densley

Jillian Peterson and James Densley, *The Violence Project*. New York: Abrams, 2021, p. 175.

Consider these questions as you read:

1. Do you believe that illegally obtained guns are the main problem in mass shootings? Why or why not?
2. How convincing do you find the argument that most Americans favor gun control? Explain your answer.
3. What counterargument could be made to the idea that background checks are essential to reducing mass shootings?

Editor's note: The discussion that follows presents common arguments made in support of this perspective, reinforced by facts, quotes, and examples taken from various sources.

There is one common denominator for all mass shootings: guns. For many Americans, this is an inconvenient truth, one that they wish would simply go away. These people work hard to convince themselves and others that guns have little to do with mass shootings. Some focus on mental illness as the cause. "Guns aren't the problem, mental health is,"[22] says gun control opponent Josey Hendryx of New York. Others blame the news media, permissive parents, or the unwillingness of society to lock up people who present a clear danger to others. Gun lovers bring up every possible explanation for mass shootings, except the one staring us all directly in the face: the nation's fascination with firearms.

Gun Laws

It is true that people have carried out killings using weapons other than guns. Baseball bats and knives have been used to kill people, but no one seriously suggests regulating or banning these items. So why, gun lovers ask, single out guns for this type of action? The answer is obvious: A gun is a much surer way of killing multiple people in a very short time than any other method. Guns are far more deadly than hammers or hockey sticks. Imagine the Parkland shooter or the Virginia Tech gunman trying to commit mass murder while armed with a knife or a baseball bat. The shooter might have been able to wound or kill one or two people, but other bystanders would have quickly seized him and stopped the carnage. The obvious answer to mass shootings, then, is to restrict who can obtain a gun and what types of guns the public can have. "The research is clear," writes the Giffords Law Center, a gun control advocacy group. "Gun laws save lives."[23]

> "The research is clear. Gun laws save lives."[23]
>
> —Giffords Law Center

For the most part, Americans agree. That is especially true in the case of assault-style weapons, which are the firearm of choice in the deadliest of mass shootings. Support for a ban on assault weapons stands at 67 percent of respondents to a 2019 Fox News survey. That is a clear majority of Americans wanting these weapons off the streets and out of the hands of mass shooters. The opposition to these guns makes perfect sense. Such guns are highly lethal, capable of shooting several rounds in a matter of seconds. They are not used for personal protection. Nor are they used for hunting or target practice. "No one needs an assault rifle," writes college journalist Mary Rudzis. "No one."[24]

The sole purpose of assault-style weapons is to kill. And they are good at that. That is why they are used by the military. It is also why they are favored by mass shooters. A shooter armed with a handgun, according to a 2017 study by Everytown for Gun Safety, kills or wounds about ten victims on average. In contrast, as reported by the public radio station NPR, "Mass shootings with assault rifles average 32 victims per incident"[25] — a figure that includes wounded people as well as those who die. Assault weapons, then, are more than three times as destructive as handguns. Given the destruction they cause, there is no good reason to allow assault-style weapons to be bought and sold in this country. A ban on these weapons would go a long way toward reducing — or maybe even ending — the epidemic of mass shootings that plagues American life.

Background Checks

Background checks are another essential tool for preventing mass shootings. The federal government and many states have laws requiring background checks for gun buyers. The idea is sound. In essence, people who have been convicted of certain crimes or who have been diagnosed with a serious mental illness are not permitted to buy a gun. Their names and other identifying information are stored in the National Instant Criminal Background Check System (NICS), a group of databases set up by the Federal Bureau of Investigation (FBI). When a customer tries to buy a gun from a licensed firearms dealer, the dealer is required to run the buyer's information through the NICS to make sure the buyer is legally allowed to make the purchase. If the buyer appears in the system, then the transaction is canceled.

Background checks, then, are a good way to ensure that firearms do not fall into the wrong hands. Americans overwhelmingly support background checks. Even among gun owners, a large majority — 83 percent, according to one recent study — supports the idea that guns should not be sold to people who are likely to misuse them. And background checks have been shown to work. The Giffords Law Center says that since 1999 background checks have prevented 3.5 million transactions that would have put a gun in the hands of someone barred from owning one.

Loopholes

Unfortunately, these laws have built-in loopholes that dilute their effectiveness. One glaring issue is that the federal law mandating background checks applies only to *licensed* gun dealers. However, millions of guns are sold each year by *unlicensed* dealers—a figure that approaches half of the gun sales that take place in the United States each year. As of 2022, twenty-one states and the District of Columbia had passed laws requiring background checks for all sales of firearms, from licensed and unlicensed dealers alike. But in much of the country, it is still easy for people to obtain weapons even when common sense dictates that they should not.

This is a huge problem. In 2019, for example, seven people were killed and twenty-two injured in a mass shooting in Odessa, Texas. Due to a mental illness diagnosis, the shooter appeared in the NICS. But the unlicensed seller from whom he purchased his weapon was not legally required to check the database, and so the sale went ahead. "That's a real loophole in the law,"[26] admitted Texas lieutenant governor Dan Patrick. It is indeed a loophole, and one that must be closed immediately.

Another loophole has to do with the effectiveness of the NICS. Not every name that should be listed actually appears in the system. The NICS relies on reporting by a variety of federal, state, and local government bodies, not all of which transmit information in a timely fashion. In 2017 a gunman killed twenty-seven people in Sutherland Springs, Texas. He had been convicted on domestic violence charges while serving in the air force and should not have been allowed to purchase

Assault Weapons Worsen the Carnage of Mass Shootings

The advocacy group Everytown USA did a study of mass shootings occurring between 2009 and 2020. One finding of the study was that mass shooters with assault weapons killed and wounded a much greater number of people than did shooters who only had handguns. About twice as many people on average are killed in a mass shooting that involves assault weapons compared to shootings that involve other types of guns, with the discrepancy being substantially greater for the number wounded. Banning assault weapons would be an important step toward controlling the carnage of mass shootings in America.

Average number of shooting victims by gun type

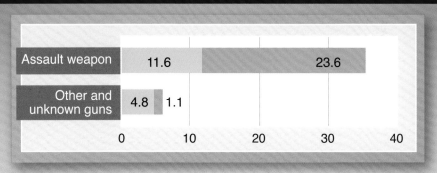

	Average number of people killed per mass shooting
	Average number of people wounded per mass shooting

Source: Everytown Research and Policy, "Twelve Years of Mass Shootings in the United States," June 4, 2021. https://everytownresearch.org.

the weapons he used to carry out the attack. However, the air force never shared the information about his conviction with the NICS. Examples like this abound. "It's a completely haphazard system," says law professor Larry Gostin. "Sometimes it works; sometimes it doesn't."[27]

No one claims that any single gun control measure is going to eliminate mass shootings. But taken together, these and other measures can have a significant impact. Making sure that *all* gun sellers perform background checks on prospective buyers is common sense. Making sure that people with a violent past cannot buy a gun is common sense. And removing military-grade assault-style weapons from all American cities and towns is another example of common sense. Nicole Hockley, who lost a child in the 2012 shooting at Sandy Hook, said it best: "There need to be background checks. . . . There is no need for thirty rounds [of ammunition]. America has a lot of guns. It always will. No one is going to take those away. All I am asking for is some common sense."[28]

Gun Control Measures Will Not Reduce Mass Shootings

"Gun control laws only affect law-abiding people who go through legal avenues to buy firearms."

—National Rifle Association

National Rifle Association, "Why Gun Control Doesn't Work," NRA-ILA, 2022. www.nraila.org.

Consider these questions as you read:

1. Do you agree that the history of gun control suggests it is ineffective? Why or why not?
2. In your opinion, how persuasive are the statistics used in this essay? Explain your answer.
3. How convincing is the argument that gun control measures serve largely to inconvenience honest and law-abiding citizens? Explain your answer.

Editor's note: The discussion that follows presents common arguments made in support of this perspective, reinforced by facts, quotes, and examples taken from various sources.

Many people advocate for stricter gun control laws to prevent mass shootings. It is easy to see the appeal of this approach. Ensure that dangerous people do not have access to weapons, and you will certainly see the number of mass shootings decline. But it is equally easy to see why this approach is completely unworkable. History, as well as common sense, tells us that gun control measures have little impact on the actions of mass shooters. Regardless of the legal barriers, dangerous people find ways to get the weapons they want. "The laws would have virtually no effect," says criminologist James Jacobs, referring to proposed new regulations on guns. "They would do nothing except maybe score points with some voters."[29]

Ineffective Laws

First, prohibitions on guns mean nothing to the criminal population. Criminals, by definition, have no compunction about breaking the law, and mass shooters are, again by definition, criminals. Mass shootings, in short, are carried out by the sorts of people who are not dissuaded by any law. The Sandy Hook shooter, for example, committed a felony when he brought guns onto the grounds of a school in his home state of Connecticut. The state's law forbidding guns on school property was completely ineffective in keeping the shooter from killing twenty-six students and teachers.

> "[Gun control] laws would have virtually no effect. They would do nothing except maybe score points with some voters."[29]
>
> —James Jacobs, criminologist

Restrictions on gun sales also mean little to a criminal who is determined to get a weapon. Mass shooters have consistently shown an ability to get their hands on firearms. Again, the Sandy Hook shooter is an excellent example. Connecticut law at the time of the shooting restricted gun ownership to people age twenty-one and older. Unable to legally buy a gun because he was still just twenty, the shooter simply helped himself to firearms belonging to his mother. Another such incident occurred in Clackamas County, Oregon, in 2012. In this case, the shooter stole a gun from a friend's house and used it to shoot three people—two fatally—at a nearby shopping mall. People who want a gun badly enough will find a way to get one.

Indeed, studies show that despite all the laws and regulations to the contrary, illegal guns are everywhere. Up to three hundred thousand guns are stolen in the United States every year, and hundreds of thousands more are purchased on the black market by people who are legally barred from owning firearms. Illegal guns are particularly common in the commission of crimes. A 2016 study carried out by the US Department of Justice revealed that about 285,000 state and federal prisoners used a gun while committing felonies. Of these, just 7 percent purchased the firearm from a licensed dealer. More laws will not alter the behavior of people who routinely ignore the laws.

> "The NICS system has only been used to disarm law-abiding citizens rather than stopping criminals."[30]
>
> —Jordan Stein, of Gun Owners of America

Gun control laws are remarkably ineffective in other ways, too. The NICS, which is designed to prevent sales of guns to bad actors, has missed an extraordinary number of dangerous people. The White supremacist in Charleston, South Carolina, who murdered nine people in 2015 should have been prevented from buying a gun. Earlier that year he had been arrested on a felony drug charge and had admitted his guilt. Federal officials, however, did not stop the sale, with tragic results. At the same time, the system flags thousands of law-abiding citizens every year. "The NICS system has only been used to disarm law-abiding citizens rather than stopping criminals,"[30] notes Jordan Stein of a group called Gun Owners of America.

Law-Abiding Citizens

Indeed, it is law-abiding gun owners, not criminals, who bear the brunt of gun laws common today. In a misguided effort to keep evildoers from getting their hands on guns, the gun owner who follows the laws is the one who is harmed. Why should a mature and responsible seventeen-year-old hunter be prevented from buying a rifle simply because of his or her age, when killers such as those in Sandy Hook and Clackamas County simply steal the guns they want? Why should a gun owner who would never carry out a mass shooting need to wait for federal approval to buy a gun, when the system misses buyers bent on mass destruction?

Nor should we expect that more regulation of firearms would be effective. In the wake of the Sandy Hook shootings in 2012, many states strengthened their gun control laws by adding measures such as background checks for buying ammunition and requiring registration of certain types of firearms. Yet the number of mass shootings has only increased. Despite the new regulations, the year 2018 set a record for the number of mass shootings. In 2017, similarly, 729 people were killed or wounded in mass shootings—far above the numbers in any given year before 2012. Mass shootings are a more significant problem today than they were before states began tightening their laws.

And the impact of gun control measures on law-abiding firearm owners is not simply theoretical. In a crime-ridden world, it is perfectly reasonable to own a weapon for personal protection. To make it harder to own a gun forces these people to sacrifice a measure of personal safety. There is no shortage of news items about people saving themselves because they owned and carried a gun. In Philadelphia in 2021, for instance, an Uber driver shot two men who attempted to rob him at gunpoint. The driver, who had a legal firearm, was not injured. More rules regulating guns will just make it more difficult for people like this Uber driver to protect themselves—and will do nothing to stop mass shooters.

Mental Health

Perhaps most seriously, focusing on gun control detracts from the real issue in mass shootings: mental health. Whatever psychiatrists and psychologists may say, no person who brings guns into a public place and begins shooting indiscriminately is of sound mind. The shooters do not benefit financially from their crime. Nor, for the most part, do they get revenge on the people with whom they are angry. And most important, no one gets away with a mass shooting. The shooters either die at the scene, whether by suicide or at the hands of police, or they are

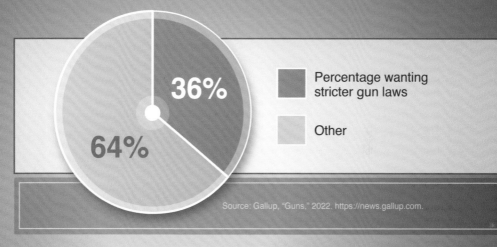

Few Americans Want Stricter Gun Laws

A 2022 survey by Gallup asked respondents what they thought about current gun laws. Just 36 percent of respondents said they wanted stricter gun laws. The remaining 64 percent said they were satisfied with current laws, wanted laws that were less strict, or had no opinion. Clearly, many Americans do not see tighter gun laws as the solution to the problem of mass shootings.

36%

64%

Percentage wanting stricter gun laws

Other

Source: Gallup, "Guns," 2022. https://news.gallup.com.

arrested and likely never again walk free. This is not the behavior of a sane person.

There are many steps that we as a society can take to deal with people struggling with mental health issues. For example, we can improve mental health screenings in high schools to ensure that teenagers who show signs of mental illness get the help they need instead of becoming mass shooters. We can be quick to remove those with a mental illness from society if they show signs of becoming mass shooters. We can increase the number of inpatient beds and the number of mental health providers. Whatever steps we take, though, the focus needs to be on mental health.

In sum, we will fail miserably if we rely on gun control measures to reduce or eliminate mass shootings. From the willingness of criminals to circumvent the law to the reasonable desire to own firearms for self-protection, gun control measures are misguided and ineffective. As Roman Catholic archbishop Charles Chaput writes, "Only a fool can believe that 'gun control' will solve the problem of mass violence."[31] Any attempt to further regulate guns will succeed only in constraining the liberty and freedom of choice of millions of law-abiding gun owners across America. In the battle against mass shootings, gun control must come to represent the road not taken.

Chapter Three

Would a Heavily Armed Population Help Reduce Mass Shootings?

A Heavily Armed Population Would Help Reduce Mass Shootings

- A heavily armed citizenry would deter potential mass shooters.
- Mass shootings could be stopped quickly and easily if ordinary citizens were armed.
- Arming teachers and other school staff will reduce school shootings.
- Some shootings have been stopped by armed guards and citizens.

The Debate at a Glance

A Heavily Armed Population Would Not Help Reduce Mass Shootings

- Most people, even if armed, would not respond quickly to a mass shooting threat.
- It is dangerous to have people carrying guns around indiscriminately.
- Arming teachers and other school staff would be foolish and wildly expensive.
- Very few shootings have been stopped by armed guards or citizens.

A Heavily Armed Population Would Help Reduce Mass Shootings

"The murderers have an incentive to disobey the law precisely because the law-abiding obey it."

—Gun researcher John R. Lott Jr.

John R. Lott Jr., "Don't Let Anti-Gun Activists Weaponize the Capitol Hill Riot," *Newsweek*, January 20, 2021. www.newsweek.com.

Consider these questions as you read:

1. The essay argues that it is time to try something new in the fight against mass shootings. Do you agree? Why or why not?
2. Do you believe that arming all or most teachers is a desirable goal? Do you think it is a realistic one? Explain your answer.
3. Which quotation in this essay best supports the essay's arguments? Why?

Editor's note: The discussion that follows presents common arguments made in support of this perspective, reinforced by facts, quotes, and examples taken from various sources.

We have tried for years to reduce the incidents of mass shootings in the United States. Thus far, though, all our efforts have been failures. Using the FBI definition of "one or more individuals actively engaged in killing or attempting to kill people in a populated area,"[32] the number of mass shootings has increased from three in 2000 to forty in 2020. Other definitions of what constitutes a mass shooting lead to the same conclusion. As a National Center for Health Research study puts it, "The number of mass shootings in the U.S. has increased exponentially since the early 2000s."[33] The number of dead and wounded has risen sharply as well. What we are doing, clearly, is not working.

If we Americans are serious about preventing these terrible tragedies, we need to start thinking beyond the usual tired and ineffective solutions. Tightening gun laws has not worked; neither has focusing on mental health. There is a solution that has scarcely been tried, however—a measure that might well prove successful. That is an armed citizenry. Imagine a country in which the great majority of adults go about their daily business with a gun strapped to their body. The image might sound absurd, even dangerous. But paradoxical as it may seem, perhaps the best solution to the problem of mass shootings is to increase the number of firearms.

A School Shooting

Consider this scenario, which has been repeated many times across the United States in the past few decades. It is an ordinary day for the students, teachers, and administrators at a school somewhere in America, when a young man carrying a semiautomatic weapon bursts through the school's front door and begins to fire. Teachers corral terrified students and herd them into closets and bathrooms. Someone calls 911. The authorities come as quickly as possible. But even if the drive to the school takes only a minute, it is already too late. The classrooms and hallways are filled with the dead and dying, and another depraved killer has made the nightly news.

Now imagine the scenario again, only this time we will make one change. The administrative assistant in the school's outer office left home that morning carrying a gun. The principal and assistant principal are armed as well, as are most teachers in the building. This is not unusual. It is standard for staff members at American schools to arrive fully armed, specifically to protect themselves and their students from the actions of an enraged gunman determined to commit murder. The gunman knows, of course, that the adults at the school are fully armed—and that they know how to use their weapons. Under these circumstances, there is a very good chance that he will not attack the school at all. Whatever his plans may be, they do not include being killed before firing a single shot.

Good Guys with Guns

And what if the gunman ignores the risk and forces his way into the school regardless? He can expect to be shot almost before he can make it through the front door. The administrative assistant, the principal, a teacher—someone would surely shoot him and eliminate the threat. Perhaps the shot kills him outright. Perhaps it only wounds him seriously enough to stop him in his tracks. Either way, disaster will be averted. The gunman will get off no shots and kill no one. The incident will be traumatizing for students and staff, of course, but far less traumatizing than it would have been in the absence of guns. As National Rifle Association executive Wayne LaPierre puts it, "The only thing that stops a bad guy with a gun, is a good guy with a gun."[34]

> "The only thing that stops a bad guy with a gun, is a good guy with a gun."[34]
>
> —Wayne LaPierre, National Rifle Association executive

Fortunately, the world is full of "good guys"—law-abiding people who reject criminal behavior and abhor mass killings. These people can be counted on to step up in an emergency. Think of the lives that could have been saved if a single "good guy with a gun" had been inside the academic buildings at Virginia Tech in 2007, when thirty-two people were murdered by a lone gunman; or at Sandy Hook in 2012, where twenty-six were killed; or in Charleston, South Carolina, in 2015, when a White supremacist murdered nine people inside a historically Black church. But there was no one to stop these massacres. Indeed, there was no legal way for an armed private citizen to have intervened. That is because, like many mass shootings, these events were carried out in places where guns were either banned or severely restricted.

It is time to allow people to openly carry weapons so that they can protect themselves and others from these heinous attacks. Consider Pennsylvania mother Meleanie Hain. Concerned about the possibility of a mass shooting at her five-year-old daughter's soccer game, she opted to bring a gun to the field. When others at the game objected, Hain held firm. "People who say, 'You do not need a gun at a soccer field' . . . I wonder if they could tell me when I will need it? That way I could just avoid that time and place."[35]

Hain was right. No one can tell when a gunman might start shooting. A school, a workplace, a nightclub, a movie theater, a concert—it is better to be prepared than to trust in luck.

This is not just idle talk. There are examples of potential mass shootings that were stopped by people with weapons. One such incident took place in 2018 in Dixon, Illinois. A former student at the town's high school, armed with a semiautomatic weapon, made his way into the high school. When he began firing, school resource officer Mark Dallas returned fire, chasing the gunman out of the school and wounding him. If not for Dallas's quick thinking—and for the gun he carried—there is every possibility that the day would have ended in tragedy. "Lives were saved thanks to the heroic actions of school resource officer Mark Dallas,"[36] noted then–vice president Mike Pence.

> "People who say, 'You do not need a gun at a soccer field' . . . I wonder if they could tell me when I will need it? That way I could just avoid that time and place."[35]
>
> —Meleanie Hain, gun owner

Arming Teachers

Arming ordinary citizens at shopping malls, sports events, and other such venues makes good sense. But when it comes to reducing mass shootings, perhaps the single most important step we can take involves the arming of school staff, notably teachers. There is widespread support for this measure. Political figures such as Donald Trump and former US secretary of education Betsy DeVos, for example, have advocated for it, and many members of the general public agree. In 2018 a CBS News survey revealed that 44 percent of Americans answered "favor" to the question "Do you favor or oppose allowing more teachers and school officials to carry guns in schools?"[37]

41

As of 2022, forty-five states allow people to openly carry handguns. In some of these states a permit is needed; in others, a permit is not required. In the remaining five states and the District of Columbia, open carry of handguns is not permitted. The data strongly suggests that Americans feel safer when people are allowed to carry handguns in the open.

Open Carry

States where handguns may not be carried openly — 5*

States where handguns may be carried openly — 45

*and the District of Columbia

Source: "Guns in Public: Open Carry," Giffords Law Center, 2022. https://giffords.org.

It is worth pondering how events at places like Parkland might have ended had teachers been armed—or whether the shooters, knowing that the teachers had weapons, might never have tried to murder students and staff to begin with. It seems self-evident that more guns in schools will eliminate or radically decrease the number of mass killings on school grounds. As one school superintendent in Ohio notes, waiting for help is often an untenable solution. In parts of his district, the nearest police station is twenty minutes away. "I'm not willing to watch my kids be murdered waiting for someone else to come,"[38] he says, explaining his support for arming the faculty of his schools.

Economist and gun advocate John Lott Jr. is one of America's foremost experts on guns. His most famous book on the subject effectively sums up his attitude toward guns and crime: The book is titled *More Guns, Less Crime*. Lott's focus is on gun violence in general, but the facts he presents fit mass shootings as well. The more guns that are in circulation and the more guns that are carried by law-abiding citizens, the safer we will be from mass killers.

A Heavily Armed Population Would Not Help Reduce Mass Shootings

"Most people in life-or-death situations freeze or shut down entirely, even the good guys."

—Mass shootings experts Jillian Peterson and James Densley

Jillian Peterson and James Densley, *The Violence Project*. New York: Abrams, 2021, p. 156.

Consider these questions as you read:

1. Do you think that armed people in public places would respond quickly and accurately to a mass shooting? Why or why not?
2. What point is the essay making about anger in American society?
3. Do you agree that arming teachers is a dangerous idea? Why or why not?

Editor's note: The discussion that follows presents common arguments made in support of this perspective, reinforced by facts, quotes, and examples taken from various sources.

In the past ten or twelve years, there has been a move toward open carry, the practice of allowing people to openly carry firearms wherever they go. Wisconsin, for example, passed an open carry law in 2011, Oklahoma in 2012, and Texas in 2016. As of 2022, nearly all states allow some form of open carry, while only a handful, such as New York and Illinois, ban open carry altogether. One rationale for these laws is protection against violence, including mass shootings. The thinking is that would-be shooters are less likely to carry out this act if they know that any random bystander can return fire and put an end not only to their plan but most likely their life as well.

It is hard to find studies to support the idea that an armed citizenry prevents violence in general or mass shootings in particular. In fact, the opposite may be true. In a 2021 study of 133 mass shootings, gun violence expert Jillian Peterson discovered that mass shootings are more deadly, not less, when an armed officer is on the scene. According to a summary of Peterson's study, "There were three times as many people killed when there was an officer on the scene who was armed."[39] Even

> "There were three times as many people killed when there was an officer on the scene who was armed."[39]
>
> —Journalist summarizing the results of a study by gun violence expert Jillian Peterson

without statistical evidence, however, it is easy to see the many downsides to this solution. There is no guarantee that in the heat of the moment the people trying to stop a shooter would be able to react quickly enough to shoot—or for that matter, would be able to determine where to aim.

A Shooting in a Theater

Consider this hypothetical scene: a crowded movie theater in which most people are armed. The theater is dark, and the film's special effects have inured the audience to the sounds of explosions, gunfire, and other loud noises. In the middle of the show, a young man pulls an assault weapon out of its case and begins to fire indiscriminately into the audience. It takes a few moments before audience members—those who were not hit in the first hail of bullets—realize that what they are hearing is not simply a part of the show. The shooter, after all, has the element of surprise on his side, and he will likely get off many shots before members of the audience are able to react. Once they do, some head for the exits or crouch under their seats, but others remain where they are, seize their own weapons from their holsters, and begin to fire.

But where are they firing? If the shooter is on the move, it may be impossible to know where he is at any given moment. Add to this the darkness, the screams of terrified audience members, and the confusion as people leave their seats. "You just smelled smoke and you just kept hearing it, you just heard bam bam bam, non-stop," remembers one survivor of a 2012 shooting in a movie theater in Aurora, Colorado. "Shots just kept going, kept going, kept going."[40] Given this degree of pandemonium, it would be nearly impossible for anyone in the audience to distinguish the shooter from the rest of the crowd. Shooters in the audience are much more likely to hit an innocent bystander than to find their intended target with their first shots.

Moreover, people are not always clearheaded—especially when they are angry. Americans have witnessed this up close during the COVID-19 pandemic. In May 2021, for instance, a passenger on an airline flight punched a flight attendant after being asked to fasten her seatbelt and wear her mask as the plane came in for a landing. In early 2022, similarly, a restaurant server in Wauwatosa, Wisconsin, was shot by a customer angry about an incomplete order. Now think about what could happen if, for example, two armed moviegoers have a dispute about seating or cell phone use during the movie. A small disagreement could easily escalate into a full-scale shooting match, leading to many injuries.

Statistics

In addition, statistical evidence casts doubt on the wisdom of arming the population. Many schools around the country have armed guards who have been trained in the safe and effective use of firearms. These guards have several responsibilities, among them representing a deterrent to anyone who might be thinking of shooting up the school. If advocates of arming the population are correct and the mere presence of guns acts to prevent mass shootings, then we would expect that vanishingly few school shootings would take place in schools where armed guards are a presence. But in fact, that is not close to being the case. Since 1999 more than 40 percent of school shootings

Mass Shootings Are More Common in Places That Allow Guns

A joint study involving Stanford University, Johns Hopkins Bloomberg School of Public Health, and the University of Massachusetts, Boston, revealed that between 1966 and 2016, only 12 percent of mass shootings involving six or more victims occurred in a gun-free zone—that is, a place where guns may not be carried or fired. The great majority of mass shootings have taken place in locations where individuals are allowed to carry guns.

Mass Shootings in Gun-Free Zones

12%

Source: "MYTH: 98% of Mass Shootings Occur in Gun-Free Zones," Gun Violence Research, 2019. www.gvpedia.org.

have taken place in buildings supposedly protected by people with guns.

Nor do statistics suggest that these guards are especially effective once a shooter does arrive. This is not to say that it never happens. There are isolated examples of armed officers staving off a shooting. But the emphasis here is on *isolated*. As the American Civil Liberties Union reports, "A study by Texas State University and the FBI examined over 160 [mass shooting] incidents, including 25 school shootings. The study found that none of the school shootings were ended by armed officers returning fire. Rather, these shootings typically ended when the shooter(s) was restrained by unarmed staff or when the shooter simply decided to stop."[41] If trained professionals are ineffective against a gunman, why would we assume that the largely untrained population would do any better?

Arming Teachers

That untrained population includes hundreds of thousands of teachers in schools all across the United States. Some people have advocated for arming teachers so they can shoot back if a gunman starts to fire. As of 2022, five states, including Texas and Missouri, have laws permitting teachers to carry guns in schools. In twenty-six other states, that decision is left to local districts, some of which have opted to allow the practice. But no state has taken steps to provide firearms and training for all teachers. Finances alone should make it clear that arming teachers is a poor idea. The cost involved in giving every teacher a firearm and training them all to use these weapons is estimated to be about one-third of the federal education budget. That is a completely indefensible expense in an era of cost cutting. In many districts, teachers are already paying for school supplies out of their own pockets, field trips have been eliminated, and maintenance on aging buildings is being deferred.

> "Putting more guns in close proximity to children is not the answer."[42]
>
> —Joan Avery, school superintendent

Arming teachers is a bad idea for other reasons as well. Even experienced gun owners sometimes fail to practice firearm safety. Witness the Alabama teacher whose gun accidentally went off in his pocket in 2019 while he was instructing a roomful of first graders. Moreover, bringing guns into classrooms may result in the guns ending up in the hands of a student. It is easy to imagine a large high school student overpowering an older or more diminutive teacher and carrying out a mass shooting—one that never would have occurred without the presence of the weapon in the classroom. As school superintendent Joan Avery explains, "Putting more guns in close proximity to children is not the answer."[42] The idea of solving school shootings by adding to the number of guns would be ridiculous—if it were not so frightening.

Source Notes

Overview: Mass Shootings in America

1. Quoted in Samuel Gaytan et al., "El Paso Shooting Updates: 22 Killed in El Paso Walmart Shooting Near Cielo Vista Mall," *El Paso (TX) Times*, August 3, 2019. www.elpasotimes.com.
2. Quoted in Simon Romero et al., "20 Are Killed in Shooting in El Paso," *New York Times*, August 4, 2019. www.nytimes.com.
3. Quoted in Merrit Kennedy and Barbara Campbell, "U.S. Charges Suspect in El Paso Walmart Shootings with Hate Crimes," NPR, February 6, 2020. www.npr.org.
4. Quoted in Michael Martin and Emma Bowman, "Why Nearly All Mass Shooters Are Men," NPR, March 27, 2021. www.npr.org.
5. Quoted in Julian Aguilar and Bobby Blanchard, "Horror in El Paso: 20 Dead, 26 Wounded in Mass Shooting at Walmart," Texas Tribune, August 3, 2019. www.texastribune.org.
6. Tammy Baldwin, "A Moment of Silence Is Not Enough—and Doing Nothing Is Not an Option," United States Senator Tammy Baldwin, June 15, 2016. https://senatorbaldwin.medium.com.

Chapter One: Could Improvements in Mental Health Care Reduce Mass Shootings?

7. Quoted in CBS News, "Jared Lee Loughner Grew Delusional in Months Before Tucson Rampage, Reports Show," March 27, 2013. www.cbsnews.com.
8. Quoted in Ann O'Neill and Sara Weisfeldt, "Psychiatrist: Holmes Thought 3–4 Times a Day About Killing," CNN, June 17, 2015. www.cnn.com.
9. Quoted in Alaine Griffin and Josh Kovner, "New Report on Lanza: Parental Denial, Breakdowns, Missed Opportunities,"

Hartford (CT) Courant, November 21, 2014. www.courant .com.

10. Quoted in Wolters Kluwer, "Study Suggests Unmedicated, Untreated Brain Illness Is Likely in Mass Shooters," Newswise, June 9, 2021. www.newswise.com.

11. Quoted in Wolters Kluwer, "Study Suggests Unmedicated, Untreated Brain Illness Is Likely in Mass Shooters."

12. Quoted in Megan Leonhardt, "What You Need to Know About the Cost and Accessibility of Mental Health Care in America," CNBC, May 10, 2021. www.cnbc.com.

13. Mayo Clinic Staff, "Mental Health: Overcoming the Stigma of Mental Illness," Mayo Clinic, May 24, 2017. www.mayoclinic .org.

14. Quoted in Jillian Peterson and James Densley, *The Violence Project*. New York: Abrams, 2021, p. 46.

15. Quoted in Jim Windell, "Are All Mass Shooters Mentally Ill?," Michigan Psychological Association, February 28, 2021. www.michiganpsychologicalassociation.org.

16. Amy Barnhorst, "Treating Mental Illness Won't Prevent Mass Shootings," MedPage Today, May 4, 2021. www.medpage today.com.

17. Quoted in Axios, "Ohio 'Incel' Charged with Hate Crime over Alleged Plot to Shoot Women," July 22, 2021. www.axios .com.

18. Quoted in Ellie Rushing, "Why It's So Hard to Force People to Get Mental Health Treatment in Pennsylvania," *Philadelphia (PA) Inquirer*, November 22, 2019. www.inquirer.com.

19. Quoted in Liza H. Gold and Robert I. Simon, eds., *Gun Violence and Mental Illness*. Arlington, VA: American Psychiatric Association, 2015, p. 91.

20. Windell, "Are All Mass Shooters Mentally Ill?"

21. Alex Pew et al., "Does Media Coverage Inspire Copy Cat Mass Shootings?," National Center for Health Research, 2019. www.center4research.org.

Chapter Two: Can Gun Control Measures Reduce Mass Shootings?

22. Quoted in Amanda Nichols, "Gun Advocates Blame People—Not Guns—for Mass Shootings," *Olean (NY) Times Herald*, February 22, 2018. www.oleantimesherald.com.
23. Giffords Law Center, "Gun Laws Save Lives," 2022. https://giffords.org.
24. Mary Rudzis, "Another Preventable School Shooting," *The Southern News* (blog), February 26, 2018. https://thesouthernnews.org.
25. Martin Kaste et al., "Most Mass Shootings Are Smaller, Domestic Tragedies," NPR, June 5, 2017. www.npr.org.
26. Quoted in Brandon Formby, "Reports: Odessa Shooter Bought Gun Via Private Sale Without Background Check," Texas Tribune, September 3, 2019. www.texastribune.org.
27. Quoted in Martha Bellisle, "Gun Background Check System Riddled with Flaws," *PBS NewsHour*, March 10, 2018. www.pbs.org.
28. Quoted in Matthew Lysiak, *Newtown*. New York: Gallery, 2013, p. 241.
29. Quoted in Lysiak, *Newtown*, pp. 237–38.
30. Quoted in David Welna, "How the National Instant Criminal Background Check System Works," NPR, November 8, 2017. www.npr.org.
31. Quoted in Patrick Novecosky, "Don't Blame the Gun, Your Eminence," *Crisis*, August 7, 2019. www.crisismagazine.com.

Chapter Three: Would a Heavily Armed Population Help Reduce Mass Shootings?

32. Quoted in John Gramlich, "What the Data Says About Gun Deaths in the U.S.," Pew Research Center, February 3, 2022. www.pewresearch.org.
33. Pew et al., "Does Media Coverage Inspire Copy Cat Mass Shootings?"

34. Quoted in Peter Overby, "NRA: 'Only Thing That Stops a Bad Guy with a Gun Is a Good Guy with a Gun,'" NPR, December 21, 2012. www.npr.org.

35. Quoted in Louis Klarevas, *Rampage Nation*. Amherst, NY: Prometheus, 2016, p. 249.

36. Quoted in Emanuella Grinberg and Amanda Watts, "This Officer Stopped a School Shooter Before Anyone Got Hurt," CNN, May 17, 2018. www.cnn.com.

37. CBS News, "Poll: Support for Stricter Gun Laws Rises; Divisions on Arming Teachers," February 23, 2018. www.cbs news.com.

38. Quoted in Kate Wheeling, "Should Teachers Carry Guns? In Many Rural School Districts, They Already Are," *Pacific Standard*, February 14, 2019. https://psmag.com.

39. Quoted in Riham Feshir, "New Research Finds Armed Officers Increases Likelihood of Mortality at School Shootings," Violence Project, February 17, 2021. www.theviolenceproject .org.

40. Quoted in Julia Jacobo, "A Look Back at the Aurora Movie Theater Shooting 5 Years Later," ABC News, July 20, 2017. https://abcnews.go.com.

41. Kendrick Washington, "School Resource Officers: When the Cure Is Worse than the Disease," ACLU of Washington, May 24, 2021. www.aclu-wa.org.

42. Quoted in John Woodrow Cox, *Children Under Fire*. New York: HarperCollins, 2021, p. 227.

Mass Shootings Facts

Numbers

- Counting a mass shooting as four or more casualties (deaths or injuries), there were 693 mass shootings in the United States during 2021, breaking the old record of 611 set a year earlier.
- The Rockefeller Institute of Government reports that there were 1,449 deaths in mass shootings during 1966 to 2020.
- According to the Rockefeller Institute of Government, there were just 12 mass shootings (four or more people killed) during 1966 to 1975, compared to 160 during 2011 to 2020.

Shooters

- According to the Rockefeller Institute of Government, 96 percent of mass shooters are men, and about 55 percent are White.
- According to Everytown for Gun Safety, one out of every three mass shooters was legally prohibited from owning a firearm at the time of the shooting.
- The Violence Project reports that 59 percent of shooters had a history of mental health issues, such as a previous hospitalization or taking psychiatric medication.
- The US Secret Service reports that 93 percent of school shooters planned their attack in advance.
- The Rockefeller Institute of Government says that the average mass shooter is thirty-three years old.
- According to Everytown for Gun Safety, in 56 percent of mass shootings, the shooter exhibited warning signs before the shooting.

Weapons

- Handguns represent 56 percent of firearms used in mass shootings, according to the Violence Project.

- The Violence Project reports that 63 percent of guns used in mass shootings were legally purchased.
- According to the Violence Project, 30 percent of guns used in mass shootings were purchased less than a month before the shooting.
- As of 2020, 32 percent of Americans own at least one gun, according to a Gallup survey.
- According to the Small Arms Survey, there are 120 guns in America for every 100 people.

Victims

- According to the US Concealed Carry Association, mass killings account for about 1 percent of homicide victims each year.
- The Children's Hospital of Philadelphia reports that there were 71 people killed in mass shootings in 2016, compared to 33,600 firearm-related homicides and suicides that same year.
- According to Gun Violence Research, about 14 percent of mass shooting victims are children or teenagers.

Related Organizations and Websites

American Psychological Association
www.apa.org
The American Psychological Association provides information about mental health issues, including the connections between mental health and mass shootings. The organization also offers information about how to cope with mass shootings in the news.

Center for Violence Prevention
https://violence.chop.edu
This website is run by the Children's Hospital of Philadelphia. It offers information about violence of all types, including mass shootings. The website provides fact sheets about mass violence, particularly school shootings, and its effects on children and others.

Everytown for Gun Safety
www.everytown.org
Everytown for Gun Safety is an organization focused on sensible gun control legislation. The group's website offers statistical information on mass shootings, as well as position papers with recommendations for steps that can be taken to reduce the number and impact of mass shootings.

Giffords Law Center
https://giffords.org
This organization was founded by former US representative Gabby Giffords, who was severely wounded in a mass shooting. It works to reduce mass shootings and other gun violence through gun control legislation. The group's website includes statistics, news releases, and position papers relating to mass shootings and gun violence in general.

Gun Owners of America

www.gunowners.org

This organization focuses on the rights of gun owners to own and carry guns without interference from state and federal restrictions. The group's website reports on legislation regarding gun control and provides articles and position papers about gun control.

Gun Violence Archive

www.gunviolencearchive.org

This website maintains a database of information about gun violence in the United States, including information on mass shootings. It breaks down shootings by type, place, and many other factors.

National Alliance on Mental Illness (NAMI)

https://nami.org

NAMI works for improved mental health across the country. Its website includes resources regarding mental health as it relates to violence in general and mass shootings in particular. The organization provides articles that oppose the idea that most mass shooters have a mental illness.

National Rifle Association (NRA)

https://home.nra.org

The best-known organization dedicated to protecting the rights of gun owners, the NRA opposes gun control measures. The group's website includes position papers and articles disputing the idea that mass shootings are primarily a problem of too many guns.

Violence Project

www.theviolenceproject.org

This website includes a database of mass shootings, along with information about how the problem of mass shootings might be stopped. The founders of the Violence Project, Jillian Peterson and James Densley, are researchers in the field of gun violence who have written extensively about mass shootings.

For Further Research

Books

John Woodrow Cox, *Children Under Fire*. New York: HarperCollins, 2021.

Mark Follman, *Trigger Points: Inside the Mission to Stop Mass Shootings in America*. New York: Dey Street, 2022.

Martin Gitlin, ed., *Mass Shootings*. New York: Greenhaven, 2020.

Carla Mooney, *How Can Gun Violence Be Stopped?* San Diego, CA: ReferencePoint, 2021.

Jillian Peterson and James Densley, *The Violence Project: How to Stop a Mass Shooting Pandemic*. New York: Abrams, 2021.

Katherine Schweit, *Stop the Killing: How to End the Mass Shooting Crisis*. Lanham, MD: Rowman and Littlefield, 2021.

Bradley Steffens, *Gun Violence*. San Diego, CA: ReferencePoint, 2020.

Internet Sources

Amy Barnhorst, "Treating Mental Illness Won't Prevent Mass Shootings," MedPage Today, May 4, 2021. www.medpagetoday.com.

Gun Violence Research, "United States Mass Shootings Fact Sheet," 2020. www.gvpedia.org.

Matt Haines, "In Wake of Several Mass Murders, Americans Once Again Debate Gun Ownership," VOA, April 14, 2021. www.voanews.com.

Mother Jones, "U.S. Mass Shootings, 1982–2022: Data from *Mother Jones*' Investigation," February 28, 2022. www.motherjones.com.

U.S. Concealed Carry Association, "Mass Shootings Facts and Fiction." www.usconcealedcarry.com.

Index

Picture Credits

About the Author

Stephen Currie is the author of dozens of books for young adults and other audiences, including many for ReferencePoint Press. Among his most recent books are *Joe Biden: Our 46th President*; *Important Black Americans in Civil Rights and Politics*; and *Systemic Racism and the African American Experience*. He has also taught levels ranging from kindergarten to college. He lives with his family in New York's Hudson Valley.